The Mansion

Written by Mary Settle

Illustrated by Amy Koch Johnson

Mary Settle lives with her husband and three daughters.
She has been blessed to be born with Cerebral Palsy and
she works to break stereotypes by educating people about
the world of disability, both through her writings and her life.
Despite doctors' predictions that she would be unable to
think, dream or feel, she has graduated high school, attended
college while volunteering at a daycare. She enjoys knitting,
bowling, swimming, and taking care of her infant.

Upon a hill far away,
was a mansion, or so they say.
In this mansion, the story goes,
lived a boy, cheeks red as a rose.

In the morning, his nurse would arouse him from sleep.
He would drive to the window and weep.
For who could love someone whose head flops around,
and whose mouth watered the ground?

Down in the valley lived a beautiful girl,
with flowing hair and eyes filled with thrill.
She was beautiful, popular, smart,
and she held the quarterback's heart.

Then one day in the late fall,
as she was walking in the hall,
Her teacher came up to her to say,
"Remember now, today's the day."

UA

He looked at her with eyes quite stern.
"Now don't forget, it's your turn,
take these books and then you will,
go to the mansion upon the hill."

The girl was nervous it was true,
truth be told, a little scared, too.
For she'd heard of the boy in the chair,
they said he was angry, mean, and didn't care.

Cold rain fell; she shook more and more,
as she climbed the hill and arrived at the door.
It opened wide; a voice said "Come in,"
through a rusty box of tin.

She walked inside on tippy toe,
wondering where she should go,
when the voice said, "Go away.
Leave the lessons for another day."

She said, "That's not what I was told to do,"
I can't go until lessons are through."
And then she heard a squeaking wheel,
that had to be from the chair of steel.

Into the light he finally came,
and in a stuttering voice slurred his name.
As the story says she didn't know,
whether to stay or if she should go.

She took a breath and stood her ground.
She'd heard he was awful to be around.
Mean and angry and hard to understand.
A boy with weak legs and a twisted hand.

But all the kids must take their turn,
the books must be brought, lessons learned.
And now she would face the boy,
who the others said had no joy.

She bent down to look in his eyes,
and what she saw there was a complete surprise.
His eyes were not angry nor mean nor bad,
just very soft and incredibly sad.

"I'm here to teach you that's true,
I don't understand all you've been through,
but I know that we will do our best,"
she said, "I'll help you pass every test."

He stared at her in such great shock,
he spoke slowly as his head did rock,
"Why don't you run away?
I'm ugly all the other kids say."

She spoke up, "Now listen here,
there's nothing ugly but their fear.
Just because you don't look the same,
is no reason to call you an awful name."

The boy was amazed, and he gripped her hand.
She was the first it seemed to understand.
They went through the lessons one by one,
and together they had so much fun.

He was funny and brave and smart,
and she came to love his kindness and heart.
And he so loved to make her smile,
for that he'd go the extra mile.

Every day the girl would go up the hill,
to see the boy had become a thrill.
She longed to hear how he thought and dreamed,
she had learned that he was more than he seemed.

And then one day she urged his nurse,
to help break his isolation curse.
Together they found a way,
so that he could go outside to play.

They built some ramps all 'round the hill,
and laughed and played 'til they had their fill.
And each day their time was done,
only with the setting of the sun.

She told the other kids and teachers, too,
about the boy and the things he could do.
But none would listen they only judged,
and their minds could not be budged.

She was angry that no one else would see,
all the things he was and could be.
That chairs, wobbly necks and twisted hands,
aren't the measure of a man.

For one should be judged by what's inside,
and not by the chair that they ride.
One should be valued for who they truly are,
and not what they seem from afar.

And slowly she began to leave behind,
others who were less than kind,
including the quarterback who was so cruel,
telling her she was being a fool.

She told him the boy in the chair,
was smarter and kinder and deserved her care.
He got angry and he made a vow,
to take revenge on the boy somehow.

So, one day the teacher told the girl,
"You dear child are a precious pearl,
you must no longer take another's turn,
up the hill you must not return."

She argued, begged, and pleaded, too,
but he only sterner grew.
"I've heard you're caring far too much,
for a boy who can't even use a crutch."

She wanted to tell him that he was wrong,
show him that the boy was strong.
But she knew he would not believe.
"But who will carry the lessons if not me?"

He said, "Don't frown and make a face.
The quarterback will take your place."
She knew that he would hurt her friend,
the one that she felt she must defend.

A storm was brewing, the sky so stark,
as she ran to the mansion in the dark.
Tears filled her eyes and made her fall,
and to the boy she did call.

The boy in the chair heard her cry,
as lightning streaked across the sky.
He rolled outside upon the path,
not knowing about the quarterback's wrath.

He found the girl drenched and in pain,
caught there in the mud and rain.
He reached down to help her stand,
when out of the dark came a hand.

The quarterback shoved the boy from the chair,
and looked at him with a frightening glare.
"Leave my girl alone," he cried.
"She doesn't like you," he lied.

"That's not true!" the girl exclaimed.
"He's not the one to be blamed,
I fell for him and love him true,
something I never felt for you."

Frustration filled the quarterback's soul.
He spoke to the boy, to hurt his goal.
"You're weak and lame, can't do a chore."
"How will anyone see you as more?"

The boy looked into the quarterback's eyes.
And could see that he believed all the lies,
but he said with a mighty act of heart.
"I can forgive you and that's a start."

Startled and suddenly filled with shame,
the quarterback realized he'd lost the game.
Knowing he could never stay,
he quickly turned and ran away.

When all the others heard the tale,
they came to see the boy as well.
They were sorry that they could not see,
all he was and all he could be.

The boy was touched but there was only one,
who could bring him warmth like the sun.
But after she kissed him his fear he hid,
as he asked her why she'd done all she did.

She looked at him with smile so sweet,
"Love is never nice and neat.
Love is a messy, wonderful gift from above,
and you always fight for the one you love."